Understanding the Demon of Poverty

Uebert Angel

Table of Contents

Chapter 1
Understanding the Demon of Poverty 5

Chapter 2
Sow your Seed don't Sow your Bread 20

Chapter 3
The Covenant of Wealth 29

Chapter 4
Tapping into the Covenant of Prosperity 36

Chapter 5
The Harvest you need when you want it 43

Chapter 6
Financial Security 62

Chapter 1

Understanding the Demon of Poverty

"The demon of poverty is more powerful than prayer and fasting combined"

"Did I just hear correctly? That cannot be correct", I thought to myself. See I had just slipped into my plush slippers and robe after a long day, and was ready to experience the finest luxury the Ritz hotel had to offer. Their guest rooms & suites offer an inspiring environment; the spacious windows let the sunlight in and provide breathtaking views of London. Each room at the Ritz, one of the most expensive hotels in the heart of London, is individual, offering its own unique welcoming atmosphere to make you do just that, feel welcome. I just wanted to pray in a relaxed place far from the madding crowd.

"The demon of poverty is more powerful than prayer and fasting combined"

The voice's dulcet tone embraced the air like a perfume of night flowers. This time I couldn't argue with it. It was all over the room and its source complimenting the hotel's turn-of-the-century origins in the subdued colors, discreet patterns and rich fabrics, complete with marble bathrooms and classic Italian furnishings. I knew it was God speaking but what he was saying was so out of my level that it was very difficult to comprehend.

I had arranged my day's prayer points in line with the millions I needed for the bank and telecommunications company we had started and here I was hearing:

"The demon of poverty is more powerful than prayer and fasting combined, DON'T PRAY FOR MONEY"

I was already on my knees to pray for money. I had set the date of receiving and all was going well until the voice came in. as I tried to understand how that could be the Lord continued;

"Don't pray for money. Prosperity is not a promise so its not subject to your prayer or fasting. It is a covenant"

I knew the vison would last long because of my ignorance on this new revelation I was receiving. It ended up lasting almost three hours with God detailing why believers are not rich and how the demon of poverty can be defeated once and for all.

God Continues

"The reason why believers are not defeating the demons of poverty is because they have an ability to manage the demon of poverty very well."

I couldn't believe what I had just heard, but I had heard that voice too many times to mistake it for anything else, I knew it was the Lord. As my mind raced to try and figure out what this really meant he continued to explain further;

"Angel, anything you mismanage goes away, but anything you manage well stays. So if you are poor you have a good management system of the demon of poverty."

That got my mind working and as the Lord continued to give detail after detail on defeating the demon of poverty through mismanaging it, a thought came to my mind. Have you ever thought about what would happen to you if you took a bottle of poison right now and drank it? You would surely die right? You'll have failed to manage your life by drinking poison, and so you lose it.

This is why in your own house you keep all harmful chemicals out of the way especially the ones you use for cleaning out of the reach of children. Why? You are managing their lives by keeping these potentially harmful chemicals out of the way.

Right now some of you are in good shape because you exercise. You are in the gym 3 times a week while somebody else may have an entirely different story to tell. They may be overweight and unfit, they have failed to manage their body in the same way that you do and lost their physical fitness. Their condition is a direct result of their failure or inability to manage their body.

Anything that you have right now is because you are good at managing it, if you are broke and don't even have two pennies to rub together its all because you have managed poverty well, you are a master in keeping poverty. **You are broke because you have managed the demon of poverty well**. Everything is based on what you are managing, there are repercussions to every thing we do.

If you were rich and you become broke, you have just failed to manage your money well. It all boils down to how you manage everything. The biggest question however is, how come you never say when somebody is broke; they are good at managing their poverty? They are better than the rich ones at managing poverty and that is exactly why they remain broke. Let me repeat; the rich are good at managing money and the opposite is true. The poor are good at managing poverty!

Let me come again before I share the other mind-blowing thing the Lord gave me in that three-hour vision. Note, you are alive right now because you manage your life well and you die because your mismanagement of life is good. It has been proven statistically that rich people tend to live longer than poor people all because they can manage even sickness through their finances well thereby prolonging their lives. So everything comes back to the level of management. How do you manage the demon of poverty? If it is on you, then you managed it well, and qualify to remain broke.

The Lord continued;

"This is exactly what I was teaching in the book of Luke"

Luke 11: 24

When the unclean spirit is gone out of a man, he walketh through dry places, seeking rest; and finding none, he saith, I will return unto my house whence I came out.

I had read this scripture many times before but somehow I knew I was in for a big surprise.
He continued;

"Notice I only said that when the demon is gone out of the man it walks through dry places, immediately when you hear that statement you think of a desert. Yet I was only pointing to the fact that the place the demon finds itself in is dry to the demon but not necessarily to you. I was not referring to a desert at all but merely pointing you to the fact that when the demon leaves, the place it goes to is a dry place for demons there is nothing to sustain it there. If the dry place was a desert then Dubai and other Arabic countries should be the poorest places on earth more than Africa because it's a desert, yet some of the wealthiest people on earth live there."

I had this all wrong. I thought the Lord was referring to dry lands and I had heard other preachers in the deliverance ministry casting out demons and sending them to 'dry places' so my mind was made up that this 'dry places' was referring to real arid lands. You can then imagine how surprised I was to note that the Lord never told us to cast out demons and send them to dry places but merely specified that the demons go there when they come out of a person. However I knew there was more to it than what I had just heard. I continued to listen, in shock but in anticipation. I knew I was about to receive a ground breaking revelation.

"Have you noticed that more prayers and fasting goes on in Africa than any other place on earth yet it remains the poorest."

Did you catch what the Lord said there? I did.

So, then he is not saying that this place is a desert, no! But that the environment in that place, is a dry one for the demon. I repeat, Jesus did not say I'm casting this demon to dry places, but that the demon will go there when it comes out, he didn't say its sent there. You still hear pastors saying; "I'm casting you now to the dry place," Jesus himself never said this is how it works.

The Shocking Truth

Understand that when the demon goes out, it cannot be sustained there, it finds itself in a place that cannot meet its needs but prefers to go back to the same place where it was cast out. Wow!

Ask yourself this profound question. What makes a demon to be sustained in a place where there is fasting, prayer, pastors, prophets, worship and prefers to back there than stay in 'dry places'? It goes back to the Christian; it knows there I can be managed well than I am managed in the dry place.

In the dry places nobody feeds it there, but in that church where you have rented a hall, you do prayer sessions, you have your choir there, the demon says, 'I can't make it in the dry place but I will go home to the Christian.' Now, think about it, the demon finds the Christian to be homely. It says in the scripture we just read;

"I will return to MY HOUSE whence I came out."

Notice here the demon just doesn't say; '**I will go back to a house**', but '**I return to MY HOUSE.**' Its so comfortable in you that it calls you **its house.** It is so much at peace in that church of yours that it calls it **its house.** I think you would agree with me that there are no DJs or MCs out there casting out demons in the clubs so the demon Jesus is talking about here came out in church and is now longing to go back home to church and to you the Christian!

Look at Matthew 21: 13 and contrast what the demon says and what God says;

And said unto them, It is written, My house shall be called the house of prayer; but ye have made it a den of thieves.

The same house that Jesus says should be called a house of prayer is the one the demon calls '**my house**'.

Church has been mismanaged so much that demons of poverty now call the people of God, the church, '**my house**'. That is something so evil that the devil sees us as his house.

This is why you find that in some churches every Sunday in and Sunday out the same demons are in church. Why are they not afraid to come back? Shouldn't they be sending each other memos to say; please don't go to that location it will not be good for you? So when you hear a demon in Africa saying; 'I'm burning, I'm burning,' know its lying, why is it coming back if there is fire there? Is the fire there more comfortable than the dryness it finds in the dry places the Lord Jesus was talking about?

Demons lie and you see the people manifesting everyday and demons crying out in loud voices that they are being tormented by the preacher's power. Some even say they are burning and then after a few minutes or seconds of fighting the preacher shouts the so obvious words 'you are free' and bam the demon is supposedly gone to the dry places. The surprising thing is come next Sunday we have the preachers casting out even more demons. So the question now remains, are these demons so dumb that they like this burning preacher so bad that they stay there Sunday in Sunday out, or is it that the 'dry places' the Lord spoke of are hotter than the preacher's power, that they need to experience the temperatures of the preacher than the 'dry places'? The conclusion is 'demons lie when they speak that's why Jesus didn't allow them to speak.

Back to Management of the demon of Poverty

The Lord Jesus told me one basic tenet of the spiritual world;

"I taught Paul so much on understanding the spiritual world that he uttered under my inspiration; 'I am not ignorant of the devil's devices" He was no so involved in revelation that he understood that in order to defeat the demonic world you have to be acquainted with how demons think and operate so you can manage it."

He continued;

"it is a spiritual rule that you can't conquer what you have no understanding of"

Equipped with that revelation I traced back my footsteps in revelation to what the Lord had spoken to me in the beginning of the open vision. I began to understand that the person who is rich right now has an ability to manage their money, in the same way that the one who never exercises stays unfit because the guy is a couch potato and can't be bothered to lift a finger. He's good at that and that is exactly why he is in that position today. You are broke right now because you are now skillful at keeping poverty its now easy for you. There is something you are doing right now that qualifies you to remain poor.

How the Demon of Poverty Operates

It is a spiritual principle that you cannot defeat what you do not understand Paul had gotten this revelation and was explaining in his letter to the Corinthians;

2 Corinthians 2: 11
Lest Satan should get an advantage of us: for we are not ignorant of his devices.

Let me repeat this because its so important. The man was pointing you to the fact that when it came to the enemy, he had gathered some intelligence. He was not going into the battle blind. Even in modern day warfare you find that different countries will send drones to spy out enemy territory. They understand the power of knowing the enemy you are fighting, but when it comes to the demon of poverty many are just throwing punches in the dark just hoping that it will land somewhere.

The demon of poverty is actually banking on your ignorance; you have not gathered any intelligence on the matter. It actually knows that even if I move out, I can still come back because you are skilled when it comes to managing poverty, there is always enough in you to feed that demon. It knows I can really enjoy there. It has realized that it's in the believer that it can be managed well; its needs are catered for there.

There are actually laws that are in you that are conducive for a demonic operation. Something that is on the inside of you that demons favour, where a demon looks at you and thinks I'm home. This is why when you start to give the demons will fight to make you broke, they will try and make you poor so you feel like giving doesn't help. You see, when you give you are the one controlling money, you are not being controlled by it and the demon of poverty knows exactly what makes you home sweet home and will do everything to keep you there.

Right now, you know your prayers never work 100 percent of the time but you still pray, it has never deterred you. When it comes to money now it's a different story, you will hear people say things like; 'I have given and given I'm now stopping,' but when it comes to prayer, you are on your knees everyday whether you get an answer or not. You need to settle it in your heart that when you give you're doing this thing until it works.

There is something else I don't want you to miss here, lets back up to verse 14 of the same chapter in the book of Luke.

Luke 11:14

And he was casting out devil, and it was dumb. And it came to pass, when the devil was gone out, the dumb spake; and the people wondered.

Remember the Lord told Joshua that;

'this book of the law shall not depart out of mouth you shall meditate in it day night and you shall make your way prosperous.' Joshua 1 vs 8

In other words, God was telling him that your prosperity has a lot to do with what will be coming out of your mouth. In fact he said to him; **"you shall make your way prosperous"**, how? When you open your mouth and speak you can control your prosperity. Proverbs 18 says; **"death and life are in the power of the tongue;"**. This is exactly why the demon of poverty will fight to keep your mouth shut and keep you dumb. The demon that controls dumb is the demon of poverty.

Without being politically correct here, you will find that most people who are dumb are poor. Very few rise up and become rich and here I mean very, very, few. There are very few dumb people in this world who are rich, they have been robbed of that ability to just open their mouths and speak. The rest of them it doesn't even need to make them dumb, but just convince them to say the wrong things. Is it not amazing how many men of God who are rich are opposed by the same people who spend hours on their knees praying to have what the man of God they are fighting has?

Their mouths have become very skilled in accommodating the demon of poverty, they are in worse position than those who are dumb and can't speak. However that's not the only way to mismanage the demon of poverty and defeat it.

The Lord weighed in;

"Do you realize that a giver's confession is stronger than a non giver's confession?"

I had not looked at it that way. The Lord continued;

"All your confessions are powered by your giving because your seed raises your faith and your faith secures the prosperity. Without the power that your confession gets from the seed you may as well sing twinkle-twinkle little star and expect a miracle"

That was humorous because the Lord had employed my words exactly. How humorous? It was just something I never expected to get from the Lord but it put a smile on my face to see that the love of the Lord is so far reaching that he can even joke with us and make us laugh.

Understand that I have tested this revelation myself and made a lot of movements in the financial world. To cut the long story short, I AM RICH Financially and that's no secret!

I want to follow closely now this next chapter as I share with some of the misconceptions that have robbed us of our God given right to be wealthy in the body of Christ with regards to sowing bread instead of sowing a seed. That has led us into managing the demon of poverty well instead of mismanaging it.

Chapter 2

Sow your Seed don't Sow your Bread

2 Corinthians 9: 10

Now he that ministereth seed to the sower both minister bread for your food, and multiply your seed sown, and increase the fruits of your righteousness;)

The Lord said to me in that vision; "do you notice that there is a difference between bread and seed?" I have read this scripture many times and like many of you reading this right now I thought I understood it, so my answer was a hasty, 'of course you give bread to the eater and seed to the sower'. But I had completely missed it, so he went on to break it down for me;

"Do you know that bread is processed seed, it no longer possesses the qualities that cause a seed to reproduce? And in my word I have never instructed believers to sow their bread only their seed. If you want a harvest sow your seed not your bread."

This blew my mind!

I have heard many Christians make this claim, that they sowed seed and never reaped, yet God in his word gave us the assurance that whenever we sow a seed we shall surely reap the harvest. He left no room for doubt, you can take it to the bank. So now I was holding the reason why many do not reap. It was so simple. Many sow bread which is processed seed and not seeds! In their ignorance of what is a seed and what is bread they have accommodated and managed the demon of poverty well.

Look at Genesis 8: 22

While the earth remaineth, seedtime and harvest, and cold and heat, and summer and winter, and day and night shall not cease.

Seedtime and harvest is a law, that means just like gravity it doesn't take a day off, it works all the time. Think about it, do you know that in the world there is still light and darkness? What about heat and cold? As surely as the sun will rise tomorrow the law of seedtime and harvest is still working, you reap whatever you sow. As long as the earth remains that law of seedtime and harvest is at work.

Galatians 6: 7

Be not deceived; God is not mocked: for whatsoever a man soweth, that shall he also reap.

If every man is reaping what they sow, then how come believers are still crying foul when it comes to sowing and reaping? Many will tell you tales of how much they have sacrificed, and it seems as if their seed never produced the harvest they desired. Yet the word of God is clear and leaves us in no doubt that whenever we sow a seed a harvest is to be expected.

Seed to the Sower and bread to the eater

The Lord continued;

"If you want a harvest, sow your seed and not your bread."

Right there I wanted to object and quote the scripture in. Ecclesiastes 11: 1;

Cast thy bread upon the waters: for thou shalt find it after many days.

His answer came before I could ask the question,

"read that scripture once more, notice I never promised a harvest right there, read it again, what does the scripture say you will find, a harvest? No! When the bible says you will find it, it is the same thing you cast on the waters to begin with. What you will find is the same

bread you cast on the waters with no increase, it was never supposed to be a seed. Bread cannot reproduce anything."

When you sow your bread the demon of poverty is not perturbed, it knows there is no ability in bread to reproduce anything and its home is safe. I stood there stunned by what I had just heard, I have read this scripture many times before and thought I understood what it meant, but my theology had just been messed up right there. To produce bread, the seed has to be ground into powder, and mixed with some other ingredients then baked. It is so easy to mistake your **bread** for your **seed**. Your bread is a product of your seed but will not give you the same result that you get from the seed when you sow it.

Notice that you can make bread out of your seed, but you can never get a seed from your bread and yet many believers sow their bread everyday. I repeat what the Lord told me in a nutshell;

"the seed is what produces and not the bread"

Many believers are digging the ground and sowing their bread and wonder why they do not receive the harvest they have been expecting. The bread though it is good for food has no capabilities of reproducing anything, you are literally throwing it away when you sow. God already knows the heart of the eater, that he will never sow anything so can never expect a harvest so he made bread to lack the ability to reproduce. That is why bread is given to the eater and not seed. Let's look at that scripture once more;

Isaiah 55: 10

For as the rain cometh down, and the snow from heaven, and returneth not thither, but watereth the earth, and maketh it bring forth and bud, that it may give seed to the sower and bread to the eater;

Notice God never said that he gives seed to eater, no! The seed is kept for the sower and bread for the eater. The two are not the same at all, the word translated as seed in that scripture is the Hebrew word *zera* it speaks of fertility, it is the same word used to refer to the seed of Abraham as in Christ. It is something that contains life within itself and it is only when you sow a *zera* seed that you can expect a harvest. The word-translated as bread is *lechem* in the Hebrew and literally means bread or grain for making it (*flour*).

So then the eater and the sower are not receiving the same thing, the sower has the ability to secure a greater harvest, each time he sows God gives the increase, on the other hand the eater only receives enough bread to see him through the day.

He is managing the demon of poverty well by living from hand to mouth and when you fail to identify your seed from your bread you fall into the same category. There is never an overflow or increase because what he has received has no ability to reproduce itself it's only good for food.

This is exactly why God instructed the children of Israel to only collect enough manna for the day only and keep none for tomorrow, they were eaters at that time they had not sown anything it was only out of his mercy that God would provide for them. Some of you hear testimonies of people who have sown million dollar seeds and you wonder how they got there because you yourself only seem to have just enough to get by. You are an eater and you are managing the demon of poverty well.

Ignorance leads to managing poverty well

The demon of poverty is ok with you giving, as long as what you putting on the alter is not a seed. Many bible believing Christians struggle in their finances and even though they seemingly observe the principles of wealth. The devil is in the detail, it's the thing you are ignorant of right now that opens the door to the demon of poverty in your life. Your ignorance makes you manage the demon of poverty well.

As I pondered on these things I could not help but wonder, "how then does the seed I intended to sow become bread and unfruitful when I go to put in the ground for a harvest"?

The answer came immediately; "The issue is many of my children look at their seed and think to themselves; I'm going to wait, one day I will sow, until that seed time lapses, for time determines what is seed and what is bread. If you stay with your seed for too long trying to make it big or just procrastinating it becomes bread and when you sow your bread it becomes a problem because all the reproductive qualities are now spent and its impossible to reap a harvest."

According to God it is a definite thing that when you sow a harvest will surely come. There is nothing wrong with the law of seedtime and harvest it works every single time, but the question is when you give, are you really seeding or you are just digging your bread into the ground and waiting for a harvest that will never come?

When you sow your seed there is a law that governs it, results are guaranteed, but if it is bread that you cast down you will never know what may come out. Many people will have that prompting and conviction in their heart that they need to sow now, but then they start to reason and question their own convictions to the point that they delay the whole process. Even the figure you end up giving is nowhere near what God had placed in your heart to begin with, so most have treated their bread as seed.

The time factor

Genesis 8: 22

While the earth remaineth, seedtime and harvest, and cold and heat, and summer and winter, and day and night shall not cease.

Now notice something here, the bible says; **seedtime and harvest**, there is an appointed time to the seeding process that is not the same for the harvest. Did you notice it says; **"seedtime and harvest"** it does not say **"harvest time"**? The reason is simple. Sowing should always be timed, it should not be rampant. It is at that time that you feel that prompting and conviction of the Spirit to sow in your heart that you ought to do it.

Obedience respects the moment of the command. If I asked you to bring me some water and you only got round to doing it the following day, you have clearly not obeyed the instruction. Yes you have completed the task but the difference is in the timing, your delay in obeying the instruction is what disqualifies you.

There is a good reason why God called it **seedtime**. When you bring it outside that time frame that God expects it, you have already broken that law, and for all we know what you are now seeding is your bread which does not have the ability to yield any harvest whatsoever. You need consistency as a sower but you need that ability to locate the right time to sow. Locate your seeding time well and your harvest can be everyday.

Even the farmers of today are very aware of the consequences of planting seed in the wrong time of the year the results can be catastrophic. A farmer that sows the wrong crop in the wrong season has just mismanaged the whole years produce and will reap nothing. It is at that time that the Spirit of God is tugging at your heart that you ought to move in obedience and put your seed in the ground. The moment you start debating the matter you are missing the seedtime and that delay is affecting your seed. The harvest God intended for you is slipping away. Before long what you are left holding on to is bread simply because you failed to time your seed.

Many have gotten into the habit of entertaining and managing the demon of poverty well simply because they have not understood these simple truths, I want to show you something that changed my life forever as we go deeper into the word in this next chapter which will detail why prosperity cannot respond to prayer and fasting.

Chapter 3

The Covenant of Wealth

"My prosperity plan is a covenant and until your part is played, I am not under any obligation to prosper you." This one statement changed my life forever. It showed me why other countries that are considered Godly are not as wealthy as those that are. This changed my life!

We know from the scriptures that financial dominion is our heritage in Christ. That means, every child of God is a candidate for wealth by redemption and has an inheritance of financial fortune in Christ. Yet many of God's people are broke and struggling to make ends meet. In their frustration they cry out to God in prayer, but even their prayers when it comes to prosperity seem to fall on deaf ears.

2 Corinthians 9: 8

"...God is able to make all grace abound toward you; that ye, always having all sufficiency in all things, may abound to every good work"

There is no doubt about the will of God or His ability to prosper you, the bible makes it very clear that believers are meant to be prosperous. Many do all night prayers trying to cast out the demon of poverty with no results to show for it. Even those who do prosper most of the time are not even sure how they got there, and cannot do much to educate the struggling masses.

2 Corinthians 8: 9

For ye know the grace of our Lord Jesus Christ, that, though he was rich, yet for your sakes he became poor, that ye through his poverty might be rich

The scriptures have already established the fact that redemption is our gateway to financial fortune. However, God empowers us for wealth through the revelation and application of the covenant. It is the revelation of covenant secrets in the Word that will launch you into financial prosperity and keep the demon of poverty at bay.

No one has the ability to empower himself for financial dominion, it is only God that can do so; and until He empowers you, you will be defeated by that demon of poverty every single time. You need to come to terms with the fact that you can only commit God on His own terms, not your own. Recognize that there is always a part you must play before you can look to God for the increase. Therefore, it is the revelation of the terms of the covenant that launches and positions men into the realms of inexplicable but undeniable wealth.

What then is a Covenant?

A covenant is a contractual agreement or deal put together by God, based on well-defined terms and sealed with an oath. The Bible itself is a book of covenants. The Old and New Testament simply mean the Old and New Covenant, and revelation is about accessing the covenants of God on every issue of interest to us, including the covenant of prosperity.

Hebrews 6:13-18

For when God made promise to Abraham, because he could swear by no greater, he sware by himself, saying, surely blessing I will bless thee, and multiplying I will multiply thee.

You see, when you enter into a covenant of prosperity because of who you are entering into the covenant with, that contract cannot be subject to the economic climate were you live or how the stock market is doing. Economic hardships; famine and drought cannot move you from your covenant place of prosperity. God himself guarantees it, this is why in the book of Malachi 3: 11 he says;

And I will rebuke the devourer for your sakes, and he shall not destroy the fruits of your ground; neither shall your vine cast her fruit before the time in the field, saith the LORD of hosts.

God himself will watch over your seed and see to it that no drought, economic depression or stock market crash will affect the seed that you put in the ground. He has an interest and obligation to see to it through the covenant but only after you do your part of the contract. You can't pray when the contract says tithe or give. You will be wasting time. A contract follows the guidelines in the contract, period!

Watch this'

Psalms 37:18-19

The Lord knoweth the days of the upright and their inheritance shall be forever. They shall not be ashamed in the evil time; and in the days of famine they shall be satisfied.

Many believers fail to recognize that prosperity is a covenant and because of their ignorance fail to appropriate what rightly belongs to them, they fall into the same trap of managing the demon of poverty the way it likes it.

Covenant people are peculiar and as long as you commit to covenant practice, you will not be subject to the demon of poverty or the economic ordeals of our time. The good news is that God has a plan in place to exempt His people. From the scriptures, we understand that every generation of people who walked in the covenant went through economic challenges triumphantly.

When you read Genesis 26 you'll see that Isaac was living in a country where there was a great famine. Everybody was suffering, the economy was very bad. But Isaac was different, he had an understanding of the covenant of prosperity watch what happened in verse 12;

Then Isaac sowed in that land, and received in the same year an hundred fold; and the Lord blessed him. And the man waxed great, and went forward, and grew until he became very great.

He prospered in a land were many had failed; he became so great that the Philistines envied him. The man was unstoppable. It seemed as if he had the Midas touch. Everything he touched was productive even against all odds. The economy of that land couldn't hold him down, he had discovered how to bind the demon of poverty. Whilst everyone else was suffering he lived in abundance. Right now if asked for you to testify many would tell of how their businesses are failing in the same environment that others are succeeding, its simply because you are blind sided by your lack of understanding and while your intentions are good you unwittingly manage the demon of poverty well.

Philippians 4: 19

But my God shall supply all your need according to his riches in glory by Christ Jesus.

Have you ever wondered why the apostle Paul would make such a bold statement, notice he says; "**my God** shall supply **your need**". Now why would he say such a thing? Its not as if the Philippians were heathens, they were brothers in Christ. When it came to the way God prospered him, Paul knew it was not the same for everyone. When he said my God, he was taking about a relationship he had with God when it came to finances which was unique to himself.

The Philippians could now take advantage of this grace because of their partnership with Paul. God could now respond to their needs in the same way he would to the needs of Paul. Paul understood the covenant of prosperity, that's why God would say to Abraham, 'I will bless those who bless you'. there is no shortcut to a world of financial fortune; it is engaging in covenant practice that empowers us to prevail in hard times.

Whoever blessed Abraham was getting blessed no two ways about it. Abraham was the one with the blessing and the anointing for wealth and God said; **'when you bless Abraham I will bless you'** in other words God was saying I will connect you to his ability to mismanage the demon of poverty when you bless him. That's a hallelujah moment right there! This is where it gets exciting, I want to show how you serve notice on the demon of poverty when you tap into the covenant of wealth, see the next chapter.

Chapter 4

Tapping into the Covenant of Prosperity

Do you realize that God never said its ok for you to not know what happens to the seed when you put it in the ground? He merely pointed out your ignorance of the process, but didn't excuse it. Do you know that you can determine how quickly your harvest comes when you sow your seed?

Mark 4: 26- 27

And he said, so is the kingdom of God, as if a man should cast seed into the ground, and should sleep, and rise night and day, and the seed should spring and grow up, he knoweth not how.

Financial dominion anchors on the covenant and law of seedtime and harvest. It is written: "While the earth remaineth, seedtime and harvest, and cold and heat, and summer and winter, and day and night shall not cease" (Genesis 8:22). With no understanding of what actually happens to the seed you sow, you never know how to get the best results possible from your seed.

There is a way for your seed to yield the best result in the shortest possible time. The reason that seeds take varying lengths of time to germinate is not because the inside of the seed takes more or less time to activate. It is simply because all seed shells are somewhat water-resistant. This is why seeds cannot grow into plants whilst they are still within the parent fruit, that hard shell prevents premature germination.

The germination time has to do with how long it takes water to penetrate and permeate the seed shell or coating and get to the inside part of the seed. Once the water reaches the inside of most seeds, they all activate and grow immediately at that point.

If you can reduce the time it takes for water to penetrate the seed shell you can dictate the germination time of your own seed. You need to understand that a seed already carries within itself the ability to reproduce after its kind, but what many fail to do is to create an atmosphere that is conducive for the seed to yield a maximum harvest.

Ecclesiastes 11: 6

In the morning sow thy seed, and in the evening withhold not thine hand: for thou knowest not whether shall prosper, either this or that, or whether they both shall be alike good.

There is a way for you to ensure the prosperity of every seed you sow, you need an ability to control how long it takes and when it will germinate. Many believers have no idea how to work the system of God or what makes their seed to produce because of that they just shoot hoping for a good outcome. All the while the demon of poverty is laughing at your futile efforts to prosper, you are still managing poverty like you want it to stay.

Understanding the power of a seed

When it is buried under the soil, the roots of the seedling grow towards gravity, while the stem grows away from it. When you see the stem of the seed shooting up and out of the ground, it is using energy and food that is already contained within the seed itself for food. At this stage it has not yet matured enough to make the most of the sunlight, but it is pushing its way up, using the energy and food within itself.

This is why when you give, the seed you are sowing should be proportional to what you really want from the plant. If the two, your seed and harvest expected are not proportional, the shoot that is trying to push its way up, will not have enough energy and food to force its way through the ground and die prematurely. It is only when it is out of the soil that it can make use of the sunlight to make food.

When you sow expecting a harvest what kind of seed are you putting in the ground? Some people will plant a two-dollar seed believing God for an award winning husband, all you will get is a two-dollar husband. There is not enough energy or food in that seed to produce the harvest required. There is nothing in your seed to push it through, the harvest you are expecting and the seed you have planted are not proportional at all. Many will just walk away thinking, 'yes, I have sowed I need a million dollar harvest now,' it will not work. The seed needs to be self sufficient in the first stages of germination before we even get to the fruit.

The Effect of Light on Seedlings

Even if a seed is planted upside down, the seedling always grows right-way up. How? Plants can actually sense gravity! (Gravity is what makes us fall back down to earth when we jump.) Inside the soil, the roots of the seedling grow towards gravity, while the stem grows away from it. This makes the roots go down and the stem come up. Once it's out, the stem also senses light, and grows towards the light. That's why, if you shine a light sideways at a plant, it starts growing sideways!

This is why it is very important what sort of light you feed your seed when it germinates. This is why doubt comes immediately when you sow, the devil now wants darkness, and will do everything he can to rob you of the light that grows your seed into a harvest. When you sowed you were acting on the Word of God and the leading of His Spirit, but then that doubt comes as if you never heard God to begin with. You have just been robbed of the light you need to bring your seed to maturity. The Bible says; "the entrance of His Word brings light", and the moment you doubt the Word you are in darkness.

Once that shoot is out of the ground, it now needs sunlight and the roots have gone deep enough to get nutrients from the soil it no longer relies on the energy it had within itself as a seed. For it to grow into a whole plant it now needs to sink its roots deep in the ground and capture the sunlight to create more energy. This is exactly where most will miss it, right after sowing you miss church and the revelation of the word in you is depleted. Right there you are denying your seed the light it relies on for growth and clouded by doubt when those who don't believe start whispering in your ears.

Right Conditions for Your Seed

There is a way for you to determine your due season in life, you just have to know how to force your seed into production. Not all seeds are the same, some plants have seeds that are hard to germinate. The biggest mistake that believers make is to just sow every seed in the same way, expecting it to produce a harvest without taking note of the conditions that will make that particular seed to yield a harvest. Some after having sown their seed will wait for years before realising a harvest.

There is a way to germinate those tough seeds. People sow but never take the time to investigate what makes a seed grow.

Mark 4: 26- 27

Jesus also said, "The kingdom of God is like a man who scatters seed on the ground. Night and day he sleeps and wakes, and the seed sprouts and grows, though he knows not how."

When people talk about seeds all they know is if I sow I will reap with no understanding of what makes the seed to produce.

If a seed is not exposed to sufficient moisture, proper temperature, oxygen, and for some species light, the seed will not germinate. In this case, the seed's dormancy is due to unfavourable environmental conditions. On the other hand, some seeds may not germinate because of some inhibitory factor of the seed itself.

Most seeds will not grow too well if they fall and land underneath the parent plant. This is because there is not enough light, water or nutrients to sustain the seed growth. It's right underneath the shadow of its parent plant and its roots will never go deeper than that of its parent plant to reach the most fertile soil. You're still stuck in that cycle of managing the demon of poverty well and are very qualified to remain broke.

This is exactly what happens to your seed when you want what the man of God has for yourself, many Christians will look at a man of God and fail to see the anointing that can deliver them but only material possessions. You are looking for your seed to produce right underneath the parent tree, and you have just missed it right there.

Even though what he has looks great to your sight that is not where your harvest is coming from. Just like a seed that falls underneath the parent plant, you will starve that seed of the light and nutrients it needs to produce when you start eyeing what belongs to the man of God. Don't get me wrong on this, you can sow into your man of God so you can get the results he has, but when you look at him and think to yourself he should give me this or that, you short circuit the power of your seed. It is God who gives the increase when you sow into life and grace upon a man. There is a way to force your seed into production in your own time. Stay with me and discover how in this next chapter

Chapter 5

The Harvest you need when you want it

'Angel I never created you to subject to the elements, you are meant to dictate your own harvest time'

I always knew that the agricultural system we have here on earth was parallel to some of the spiritual principles in the bible, but this I never knew was possible. I mean God was talking science, talk about coming down to our level this was it. Let me break it down for you it will make sense in a minute.

Scarification of seeds

Scarification in botany involves weakening, opening, or otherwise altering the coat of a seed to encourage germination. Scarification is often done mechanically, thermally, and chemically. The seeds of many plant species are often impervious to water and gases, thus preventing or delaying germination. Any process designed to make the testa or seed coat more permeable to water and gases (and thus more likely to germinate) is known as scarification. Scarification, regardless of type, works by speeding up the natural process that normally makes seed coats permeable to water and air.

Mechanical Seed Scarification

This involves breaking or weakening the seed coat and can be carried out using sandpaper or a file to abrade the seed coat, or using a knife to nick the coat, or using an hammer to crack the seed coat for allowing water to enter. This treatment works well for larger seeds. Smaller seeds may be rubbed between sheets of fine grit sandpaper. If the seeds are too small to see the progress, a different method such as soaking should be used.

Seeds that have been known to take weeks to germinate, have done so overnight after mechanical scarification. Damaging the outer coat of the seed will let moisture in quicker for seed germination. Scarification will shorten the waiting period for your harvest

Many don't know this but your seeds were designed to be abused. Mother Nature is not kind to a little seed. In the wild, a seed can expect to encounter harsh heat and cold, very wet or dry conditions and may even need to survive the acid-filled digestive tract of an animal. In short, seeds have developed over millions of years with defenses to survive awful conditions. But in your modern day garden, a seed is relatively pampered yet we expect it to yield a harvest in the same way as ones that have suffered abuse.

It is only when you give a seed for a specific purpose, and you know in your heart and can see that there goes my seed, it has just paid for the airfare of my man of God or maybe fuelled his car, for example. You got to understand that the seed needs to be spent and you need to observe the man of God spending it! You know that your seed has been spent, that seed has been abused and goes into the soil scared, the protective coat that normally delays germination and the permeation of water has been broken down. Your seed has just gone through scarification, you don't have to wait on the elements to speed up your harvest, you have just forced the seed into production.

Chemical Scarification

This involves the use of one or more chemicals to promote germination. It can involve imbibing or soaking seeds in precisely concentrated acidic or basic solutions for varying amounts of time. Chemicals such as sulfuric acid or even also be achieved through the use of nutrient salts such as potassium nitrate. This process was developed to try and mimic what happens to a seed in the wild but do it in a controlled environment.

Some seeds won't germinate unless they have passed through the stomach of an animal. Sometimes you have to see your seed being spent by those whom you sowed into. This is a chemical form of scarification. The germination of most seeds that require this treatment will be aided by soaking briefly in an acidic solution, such as glacial acetic acid.

There are certain types of seeds that need to go through the digestive system of an animal in order to break down the germination inhibitors within the seed. The intestines of animals have the ability provide the right kind of acidity to do the job and it's not every animal that carries this ability. Some animals will have a low level of acidity in their gut and that seed will come out the same condition it went in. That particular seed will only germinate after it has been exposed to the right kind of chemical environment and you will struggle to bear any fruit in that area until you recognize the environment with right level of acidity for your seed to germinate.

In Brazil there was a horticultural doctor who discovered that some seeds even after being swallowed and processed by a tortoise remained dormant, but when the same seed was eaten by a deer the germination inhibitors of the seed were broken down and germination would be quicker. After research and scientific study they discovered that the enzymes and the fluids in the intestines of the tortoise where more alkaline and less acidic compared to that of the deer. So then whole process is not just about the seed going through the gut of an animal but it matters which kind of animal gets to eat the seed.

That means that when you sow your seed you need to know, that as for this kind of seed, I need to sow it here because I can see the result of the acidity in this particular man of God, so I can expect his anointing to have the ability to break down any inhibitors that come with my seed. There are men of God whose grace and anointing is more alkaline than acidic, meaning the harvest will take longer. Just because you sowed into a man of God doesn't mean the result is automatic. No! Your seed may have just been eaten by the wrong kind of animal. This is why many are frustrated because they think they have followed the Bible to the letter with no results to show for it.

I remember ministering to one particular brother and the Lord revealed to me prophetically that he had been praying for a house, the house that he wanted was in one particular suburb called Norton and the Lord had granted his request. Just as I was about to deliver the good news the Lord stopped me right in my path. He said, "the anointing I gave you is too great to give the man a house in Norton, tell him you are upgrading him to a different town." When you are sowing a particular kind of seed it's important to note whether or not the anointing you are sowing into has the ability to reproduce that thing.

Thermal Scarification

Thermal scarification can be achieved by briefly exposing seeds to hot water, which is also known as hot water treatment. A seed only germinates when water has entered inside, that's why we boil beans. When you boil the bean it cracks the outer coat and water gets inside and softens it. Now water is representative of the word, the bible says;

Psalm 34: 18

The Lord is near to the broken hearted and saves those who are crushed in spirit.

That's a place of dependency on the Lord and total surrender. Secondly you have to believe that seeding works, because the bible says; "anything that is not of faith is a sin". Your heart has to agree with it. And if it is of faith then you need to consistently stand on the word of God, the word of God is that water that gets into the seed and initiates the harvest you want.

Pre Soaking

For some types of seeds, they actually contain germination inhibitors that are designed to prevent a seed from germinating inside the fruit. So no financial harvest comes into your bank account when you haven't sown it. These inhibitors must be leached away before a seed can germinate. In nature with rainfall can facilitate the removal of the inhibitors, but this process can take some time. But when you soak your seeds, this process is sped up.

This simple procedure exposes the seed embryo to moisture, which is the primary impetus for making it grow. Soaking seeds before planting helps you to break down the seed's natural defenses against what it expects from Mother Nature, which then allows it to germinate faster. Another reason is that while Mother Nature actively assaults seeds, she also gave those seeds an internal gauge to help them know when they should grow. For most seeds, moisture levels play a big role in alerting a seed to optimal grow times. By soaking the seeds, you can quickly boost the moisture content around the seeds, which signals to the seed that it is now safe to grow.

This is normally done to those seeds with a thick coat, when you are expecting a life changing harvest and you are putting this aside to sow it as a sacrificial seed. You are soaking it! Before you can plant it! You are not spending it, but you are taking your time. This is the kind of seed that can change God's mind concerning your case.

2 Kings 3: 27

Then he took his eldest son that should have reigned in his stead, and offered him for a burnt offering upon the wall. And there was great indignation against Israel and they departed from him, and returned to their own land.

The king of Moab sacrificed his eldest son when he saw that he was losing in battle, he had understood the power of a sacrificial seed. Israel had a prophetic word from God Himself to say they would be victorious but when God saw the king's sacrifice he changed his mind and his own people lost that battle. Elisha the prophet had told them that God would deliver the Moabites into their hands but the king's sacrificial seed turned the whole thing on its head.

When you give sacrificially in this manner you have broken down the hard shell of your seed and the results are instant. This is a seed you have been putting away, your sweat and tears have gone into it and it could have potentially done other things for you but you choose to make it your seed. In the same way, the king of Moab had invested a lot of time and energy in grooming his eldest son who was the heir to his throne. His wisest advisors would have tutored the boy, he would have had a chance to sit in the king's court and learn the political system of the land. When push came to shove and he needed results and see things change immediately this became his seed. He had just planted a pre-soaked seed and results were felt instantly.

Tithing

This is the covenant foundation for financial fortune. It is also the first fruit that makes the balance meaningful. As it is written:

Malachi 3: 10

Bring ye all the tithes into the storehouse, that there may be meat in mine house, and prove me now herewith, saith the Lord of hosts, if I will not open you the windows of heaven, and pour you out a blessing, that there shall not be room enough to receive it.

Remember the demon of poverty is not subject to your fasting and prayer this is why God makes this his part in the covenant of prosperity to rebuke the devourer on your behalf.

Malachi 3: 11

And I will rebuke the devourer for your sakes, and he shall not destroy the fruits of your ground; neither shall your vine cast her fruit before the time in the field, saith the Lord of hosts.

Notice something here, God himself will rebuke the devourer on your behalf, it was never your part! Just do what you are supposed to do and leave God to do what you can't. But there is something else I don't what you to miss, you see the word translated as rebuke there is the Hebrew word gaw-ar which means to chide that is to reprimand or to lambaste it's the same word that is used when Moses parts the Red sea, the bible says he rebuked the sea, and it dried up.

Psalm 106: 9

He rebuked the Red sea also, and it was dried up so he led them through the depths, as through the wilderness.

When you become a consistent tither even those difficult times that trouble the rest of the population will not touch you. You are no longer subject to the elements, you become immune to the recessions and financial depressions of this world. All financial testimonies in the body of Christ are rooted in consistent tithing.

It is also written: "Honour the Lord with thy substance, and with the first fruits of all thine increase: So shall thy barns be filled with plenty, and thy presses shall burst out with new wine" (Proverbs 3:9-10).

For instance, Abraham was a tither and he became a possessor of heaven and earth. For us to access the blessings of Abraham, we must do the works of Abraham. Remember, Christ redeemed us from the curse of the law to connect us to the blessings of Abraham. All we need to do is walk in his steps to flow in the kind of blessings that he experienced (Genesis 14:19-20; John 8:39; Galatians 3:13-14, 29).

Tithing remains a covenant obligation for financial fortune if you are serious about being rich God's way you need to tithe. You must understand that your tithe is not a donation; rather, it is part of our spiritual responsibility. The truth is, any believer who is not a tither will remain a financial struggler. This is because it is impossible to be in command of financial fortune without being a tither. You will always be subject to the demon of poverty and notice in Malachi God said; I will rebuke the devourer, He takes that responsibility upon himself because your prayer and fasting cannot do it.

Kingdom-promotion giving

We are instructed in scripture not to go into God's presence empty-handed. This is because God takes cognizance of every offering we bring when we are in worship. This is one of the requirements for walking in financial dominion. As it is written:

Exodus 35:3-5

Ye shall kindle no fire throughout your habitations upon the sabbath day. And Moses spake unto all the congregation of the children of Israel, saying, This is the thing which the Lord commanded, saying, Take ye from among you an offering unto the Lord: whosoever is of a willing heart, let him bring it, an offering of the Lord; gold, and silver, and brass

it is important to understand that our seed is not a financial donation to 'help' God, the church, the ministry or the minister. Rather, it is a spiritual transaction that provokes the release of financial fortune in the ultimate, among others. The good news is, the covenant has never failed and it will not fail in our lives. All we need to do, therefore, is to play our part by engaging the covenant so as to commit God's integrity to perform in our lives.

But how do you make sure you have dealt with all inroads of the enemy into your life? How do you make sure you have mismanaged the demon of poverty and managed the covenant well? This is what we are dealing with in this next and final chapter.

Chapter 6

Financial Security

'Do you realise that I don't have the ability to stop Satan from ransacking certain areas of your life?'

I thought I had heard this statement incorrectly and immediately I interjected; **'you mean to say there are certain areas that you wont stop the devil, right?'** His answer hit me just as hard as his opening statement, I was not ready to hear things like this.

'I mean I cannot do it even if I wanted to stop him, I cant.'

Like most of you right now, I was ready to quote the King James version of my Bible to make my case of how powerful God is, how the devil is far inferior to him and how all things are possible. Before you get confused let me take to the scriptures that he showed me that day. Do you realise that as a believer you can short circuit the power of God in your life?

Genesis 39: 2- 3

And the Lord was with Joseph, and he was a prosperous man, and he was in the house of

his master the Egyptian. And his master saw that the Lord was with him, and that the Lord made all that he did to prosper in his hand.

Potiphar knew beyond the shadow of a doubt, that the hand of the Lord was upon Joseph the results were undeniable. It seemed as if Joseph had the Midas touch, the bible actually says; **'the Lord made all that he did to prosper in his hand.'** and when the bible says that; *'his master saw that the Lord was with him,'* The Hebrew word translated 'saw' is *raah* it means to experience or discern.

Potiphar knew that the hand of the Lord was on Joseph by experience, he had seen the results in his own house. He was so convinced that he took all his possessions and put them in the hands of Joseph. He understood that anything he put under Joseph's charge would carry the same blessing.

Genesis 39: 4

And Joseph found grace in his sight, and he served him and he made him overseer over his house, and all that he had he put into his hand.

Some of you right now will look at your family and you can see the hand of the Lord on your kids or your finances. There is no doubt in your mind that God is with you but still the enemy seems to find a way to ambush you in some other areas. Even with all the wisdom that God had given Joseph it was only a matter of time before the enemy came into the household of Potiphar and wreak havoc.

With the anointing and the grace that the Lord had placed upon Joseph, running the household of Potiphar should have been a piece of cake. I mean the guy had the ability to run a country and here he was managing the household of one Potiphar. But how could the devil enter where God was working and succeed?

Genesis 39: 9

There is none greater in this house than I; neither hath he kept back any thing from me but thee, because thou art his wife; how then can I do this great wickedness, and sin against God?

The moment that Potiphar committed his household to Joseph everything in that place was working like clockwork. But there was one thing that was outside the control of Joseph, the wife of Potiphar. Right there was a window of opportunity that allowed the enemy to come in and cause destruction. Everything that was in the house was under Joseph's charge, the fields and businesses were all controlled by Joseph and the enemy couldn't touch those. He never heard one bad report from there.

Joseph had no authority over the wife of Potiphar, the grace and anointing that was working in the fields to bring prosperity and in the house to bring harmony couldn't work on the wife of Potiphar, she had not been put under that anointing.

Right now anything that you have not committed to the Lord, is a window of opportunity for the enemy to come in and use to destroy you. God will never force his way into any area of your life. God's plan for you is for you to have nothing broken and nothing missing. Right now you are saved, you know you are going to heaven but when it comes to your finances you're just as broke as you were before you received Christ or worse.

The anointing that healed you and keeps your family together doesn't seem to work when it comes to the area of your finances. You have committed all things to the Lord except the area of your finances and God has no right to intervene when the demon of poverty is on the offensive. Just like Potiphar you have left a window that the enemy is able to creep in and destroy everything else. Paul wrote to the Colossians urging them to do everything in the name of the Lord.

Colossians 3: 17

And whatsoever ye do in word or deed, do all in the name of the Lord Jesus, giving thanks to God and the Father by him.

Paul is instructing to do everything in the authority or the character of Christ not just the things they feel are necessary for the Lord to be involved in but all things in word or deed. He was saying there should be nothing you do without acknowledging the Lord. In all your ways acknowledge him and he will establish it.

Romans 10: 9

That if thou shalt confess with thy mouth the Lord Jesus, and shalt believe in thine heart that God hath raised him from the dead, thou shalt be saved.

The Greek word translated as saved is *sozo* it just doesn't mean salvation from hell, no! It means to be made whole every part of your being and area of life. Even though this is the will of God for you this is far from the reality most are experiencing.

You see, when you become a faithful tither and a giver you have just given the Lord jurisdiction over your finances. When you read the book of Malachi he actually points us to this fact.

Malachi 3: 10- 11

Bring ye all the tithes into the storehouse, that there may be meat in mine house, and prove me now herewith, saith the Lord of hosts, if I will not open you the windows of heaven, and pour you out a blessing, that there shall not be room enough to receive it.

And I will rebuke the devourer for your sakes, and he shall not destroy the fruits of your ground; neither shall your vine cast her fruit before the time in the field, saith the Lord of hosts.

It is when your finances are committed to the Lord through your Tithing and offering that he has the authority to rebuke the demon of poverty on your behalf. Until you commit that area of your life to God yes you will go to heaven but you will live your life at the mercy of the demon of poverty. You will be stuck managing the demon of poverty in the same way you have always done, keeping it cozy in your house. Always longing for more and never having enough. The Lord's hands are tied when it comes to your finances until you choose to hand them over.

Are you ready for money to follow you? If the answer is yes, then remember the words of the Lord to me in the three hour vision;

"The demon of poverty is more powerful than prayer and fasting combined!"

Prosperity is a covenant. It is a contract. It only responds to you fulfilling your end of the contract and then that gives God the switch to flip the spiritual button of money and wealth in your favour.

Now, let's defeat the demon of poverty!